THE WORLD AT WAR
WORLD WAR II

Children During Wartime

Heinemann
LIBRARY

. . . . Brenda Williams

www.heinemann.co.uk/library

Visit our website to find out more information about **Heinemann Library** books.

To order:
☎ Phone 44 (0) 1865 888066
🖹 Send a fax to 44 (0) 1865 314091
💻 Visit the Heinemann Bookshop at www.heinemann.co.uk/library to browse our catalogue and order online.

First published in Great Britain by Heinemann Library, Halley Court, Jordan Hill, Oxford OX2 8EJ, part of Harcourt Education.
Heinemann is a registered trademark of Harcourt Education Ltd.

Editorial: Andrew Farrow and Dan Nunn
Design: Lucy Owen and Tokay Interactive Ltd (www.tokay.co.uk)
Picture Research: Hannah Taylor and Sally Claxton
Production: Duncan Gilbert

Originated by Repro Multi Warna
Printed and bound in China by WKT Company Limited

The paper used to print this book comes from sustainable resources.

ISBN 0 431 10380 1
10 09 08 07 06
10 9 8 7 6 5 4 3 2 1

British Library Cataloguing in Publication Data
Williams, Brenda, 1946–
    Children during wartime. – (World at war. World War II)
    1. World War, 1939–1945 – Children – Great Britain – Juvenile literature
    I. Title
    940.5'3161
A full catalogue record for this book is available from the British Library.

Acknowledgements
The publishers would like to thank the following for permission to reproduce photographs:

Corbis pp. **5** (Hulton Deutsch Collection), **7 bottom** (Lucien Aigner), **11 top** (Hulton Deutsch Collection), **12** (Bettmann), **14** (Bettmann), **15 bottom** (Bettmann), **16**, **19 bottom** (Bettmann), **19 top** (Bettmann), **21**, **23** (Bettmann), **24** (Hulton Deutsch Collection), **25** (Hulton Deutsch Collection), **27 top** (Bettmann), **27 bottom** (Bettmann), **28** (Hulton Deutsch Collection); Getty Images pp. **6** (Time & Life Pictures/Hugo Jaeger), **8** (Hulton Archive), **9** (Hulton Archive), **18** (Hulton Archive), **20** (Hulton Archive); Imperial War Museum pp. **7 top**, **10**, **26**; Topfoto.co.uk pp. **11 bottom** (HIP/The Lord Price Collection), **22 left** (Public Record Office/HIP), **22 right**; Topham Picturepoint pp. **15 top**, **17**; TRH Pictures p. **4**.

Cover photograph of a child after a German air raid on London, August 1940, reproduced with permission of AKG Images.

Every effort has been made to contact copyright holders of any material reproduced in this book. Any omissions will be rectified in subsequent printings if notice is given to the publishers.

CONTENTS

Some words are shown in bold, **like this**. You can find out what they mean by looking in the glossary.

PREPARING FOR WAR

World War II began in September 1939. For the next six years, children in many nations grew up during wartime. Millions of children lost their homes and families. Many thousands of children lost their lives.

During the 1930s, children in Europe and Asia had already experienced war. There was a bitter **civil war** in Spain, China was attacked by Japan, and Abyssinia (now Ethiopia) was attacked by Italy. War hurt many children, through fear, injury, homelessness, and loss of family. Children were also victims of religious and racial **persecution**, especially in Germany. There the **Nazis** came to power and began a campaign to drive out **Jews**. In Europe and America, there was talk of a new world war.

War in Poland

On 1 September 1939, war became horribly real for Polish children, when German armies invaded Poland. Polish soldiers fought to defend their country. But in this new war, children and other **civilians** were in as much danger as the soldiers. Many were killed as German planes dropped bombs on homes and schools, while tanks smashed through villages and cities. Many children fled from their homes to become **refugees**, but there was no escape. Poland was defeated.

On 3 September 1939, families in Britain heard prime minister Neville Chamberlain's grim radio broadcast: Britain was at war with Germany. Newspapers carried the stark headline, "WAR". Cinema newsreels showed film of armies on the move. Across Europe and in the United States, Canada, and Australia, families waited for war news.

▲ Children were among the many refugees who packed roads in their efforts to escape to safety. But by 1940, millions of children like these in Poland were living under Nazi rule.

3 September 1939

Britain and France go to war with Germany, which has attacked Poland. Britain is supported by the Commonwealth countries.

April–May 1940

Germany invades Norway and Denmark, then Holland, Belgium, and France.

July–September 1940

With no allies left in Europe, Britain's Empire fights alone.

Ready for war

In Britain, children had noticed war preparations before September 1939. Fathers and uncles who were former soldiers "in reserve" were ordered back to the Army. Air force planes practised overhead. Navy ships left port to patrol the oceans and protect trade.

The United States was still at peace in 1939, though most people supported Britain and its Commonwealth **allies**. American children followed the war news over the next few months. In 1940, they learned of the fall of France and the **Battle of Britain**. In 1941, they heard of the invasion of the Soviet Union (USSR, or Russia) by German armies. Then, on 7 December 1941, Japan attacked the US naval base at Pearl Harbor, in Hawaii. This surprise attack shocked Americans and brought the United States into the war. All Americans knew this was now their war too.

▶ Children in London watch an **air raid shelter** being built in 1938. People feared that a new war would bring "terror-bombing" on a scale not seen before.

22 June 1941	7 December 1941	11 December 1941
Germany invades the Soviet Union.	Japanese naval planes attack the US naval base at Pearl Harbor. The United States enters the war.	Germany and Italy declare war on the United States.

Signs of war

Although there was no TV or Internet in the 1930s, children knew about war preparations. Adults talked about war. Newspapers had photos of Europe's leaders holding crisis talks. Cinemas showed world news on newsreels (short films), and audiences saw Hitler making boastful speeches to vast crowds in Germany. By 1940, children sat with their families around the wireless (radio) to listen to British prime minister Winston Churchill's words of defiance, or to the "Fireside Chats" of US President Franklin Roosevelt.

Most people got war news from the radio. Families also received government leaflets, telling them how to cope with **air raids**, the **blackout**, and **rationing**. Children in Britain got used to putting on gas masks, covering lighted windows at night with dark blackout curtains, and clearing up after air raids. At school, they pinned flags on maps to show where battles were fought. They read letters from fathers, uncles, and brothers stationed in faraway places. Everyone wondered how long the war would last.

▶ Almost every child knew about Germany's leader, Adolf Hitler. Some made jokes about his little moustache and Nazi arm salute – but Hitler was no joke. Ever since 1933, when the Nazis took power in Germany, Hitler had made news. By 1940, Germany's Führer (leader) was celebrating the defeat of France. He seemed to be winning the war.

Eyewitness

Many people feared bombing would destroy whole cities. David Ross (age 14) thought so, from what he had been taught.

"It was assumed London was going to be razed [smashed] to the ground. I was convinced of this myself because I was in the Scouts and I had my Civil Defence badge ..."

◀ A mother in a gas mask holds her baby in a baby-mask (which had a hand pump to supply air for the baby). Some 38 million gas masks were issued in Britain. Everyone, including children, had to practise gas drills and keep their gas masks handy. In the end, however, poison gas was not used in Europe.

In the News

"Always keep your gas mask with you – day and night.
Learn to put it on quickly.
1. Hold your breath.
2. Put on mask wherever you are.
3. Close window."
These instructions told people what to do if the enemy dropped poison gas bombs. They come from a poster issued in 1939 by Britain's Ministry of Home Security.

▼ American students at a school in Long Island, New York, learn about the war in Europe, in 1940. The United States would not join the war until the following year.

CHILDREN ON THE MOVE

Many families were forced from their homes by the war. They fled from the fighting and became refugees. In Britain, thousands of children were moved from the towns to escape the bombs. In America, many Japanese-American families were locked up – because of fears they might be spies.

Evacuation

Evacuation began before the war. In 1938, many governments offered refuge to Jewish children from Germany, to save them from Nazi persecution. Between December 1938 and the beginning of September 1939, about 10,000 children were brought to Britain under the *Kindertransport* (child-moving) scheme. Many who left their parents never saw them again. After the outbreak of war, many British children also left home as **evacuees**. They were sent away from the cities to new homes in the country, where they would be safer.

Refugees

In May 1940, German armies raced into France. French roads were jammed with refugees desperate to escape the shelling and bombing, fleeing with whatever they could carry. Most were women, children, and old people. When the fighting stopped, most returned home to live under German occupation. Others found new homes in the south of France, which was not occupied by the Germans.

In the News

In 1938 a German official in Hamburg wrote that "Jewish children emigrating on group transports must submit documents ... certifying that they owe no taxes ..." The Nazi laws about Jews applied even to children, and Jewish families seeking to leave Germany had to hand over all their money.

▲ For Jewish children leaving Germany in 1939, countries such as the USA, Canada, Britain, Palestine, and Australia offered a refuge from the Nazis – but most had to leave behind parents and friends.

21 November 1938	2 December 1938	September 1939
The British government offers German-Jewish children homes, to escape persecution by the Nazis.	The first Kindertransport ship lands Jewish children from Germany at the English port of Harwich.	Britain begins a mass evacuation of city children to the country. Thousands also go to Australia, Canada, the United States, New Zealand, and South Africa.

Effects of the Pacific war

Children in Asia also became refugees, especially in China, which had been invaded by Japan in 1937. By 1941–1942, fighting had spread to Malaya, Burma, Indonesia, and the Philippines. In the United States, anti-Japanese feeling led to the imprisonment of more than 120,000 Japanese-Americans living in California and other West Coast states. They were held in remote internment camps, under guard. The government thought Japanese-Americans might spy for, or help, Japan. In fact, almost all were loyal Americans.

◀ The US Government reacted to the Pearl Harbor attack of 1941 by bringing in a new law. It banned people of Japanese **ancestry** from living or working in certain areas. Most of the people sent to internment camps were US citizens, but they were forced to live for up to four years behind barbed wire.

Eyewitness

Californian teenager Louise Ogawa (age 16) wrote from an internment camp in Arizona to a San Diego librarian, Clara Breed. Clara tried to keep up the spirits of Japanese-American internees like Louise by writing to them.

"When I stop to think how the pilgrims [the Pilgrim Fathers of 1620] started their life, similar to ours, it makes me feel grand ..." Louise told Clara. But she "wished with all my heart that I could go back to San Diego".

May 1940	1941	1942
Thousands of families flee from their homes as Germany invades Holland, Belgium, and France.	Millions of Russians become refugees to escape German armies invading the Soviet Union.	The US government opens the first internment camp to hold Japanese-American families.

Life as an evacuee

Evacuation in Britain began in 1939. Between September 1939 and August 1940, some 1.4 million people were on the move, and about half were children. Some went abroad, but most were sent to the country. Special trains left the cities, with children waving goodbye to tearful mothers. New homes, or billets, for evacuee children were selected by **billeting officers**.

The experience was an eye-opener to children and their host families. Some country people complained that the "townies" (many from poor families) were dirty, did not eat "nicely", and had no proper shoes or clean underwear. Some town children did not think much of the country. "I miss the park," wrote one seven-year-old, while another missed electric light, telling his parents gloomily "we have candles here". But others enjoyed the fields and fresh air, and were quite sad to leave when they returned to their parents.

▶ In the spring of 1940, a London policeman checks a little evacuee's label, to make sure she is put on the right train. People were sad to see children go, but hoped they would be safe out of the cities. British TV presenter Michael Aspel, a wartime evacuee, remembered being given sweets and nuts by smiling shopkeepers as he and his school friends walked to the station.

Evacuees

For many British children, evacuation meant their first long train journey. More than 750,000 unaccompanied children were billeted in September 1939. Locals called the newcomers "townies" or "skinnies". Gradually children returned home, and by January 1944 fewer than 200,000 were still living apart from their parents.

CHILDREN ON THE MOVE

In the News

On 17 September 1940, the passenger ship *City of Benares* was torpedoed in the Atlantic by a German submarine (U-boat). The *Liverpool Daily Post* newspaper reported "294 drowned in Nazi outrage". Among the dead were 83 child-evacuees on their way to Canada. The newspaper listed the victims and told its readers, "a storm added to the tragedy ... children trustingly obeyed orders as the ship was sinking". Two girls clung to an overturned lifeboat, before being rescued.

▲ This picture was meant to show that being away from home was fun. Most evacuees did have fun, though one boy said he missed the sink at home, because "we have to go outside to wash here".

Eyewitness

A typical evacuee from London left home with "a gas mask in a tin box ... a haversack crammed with sandwiches and apples ... brown paper parcels with more sandwiches, chocolate, spare socks ..." Like all evacuees, the child had a label with his or her name, home address, school, and destination. He or she carried a small suitcase and in the other hand, "a wad of comics".

LEAVE THIS TO US SONNY — <u>YOU</u> OUGHT TO BE OUT OF LONDON

MINISTRY OF HEALTH EVACUATION SCHEME

▶ British government posters stressed the importance of children leaving bombed cities for the safety of the countryside.

AIR RAIDS

AIR RAIDS

World War II was the first war in which mass air attacks destroyed cities. Cities in Europe and Japan suffered heavy bombing. For many children, air raids became part of daily, and nightly, life.

Britain was bombed by German planes in 1940–1941. This bombardment became known as the **Blitz** (from the German *Blitzkrieg*, meaning "lightning war"). There were more air raids in 1944, this time by V-1 flying bombs and V-2 rockets. From 1942, German cities were heavily bombed by British and American planes. In the Pacific, Japanese planes bombed some Australian towns, while American bombers attacked Tokyo and other Japanese cities.

▶ Air raid shelters were designed to protect people from bomb-blasts. This is a public shelter in New York, in the United States. Although the United States prepared for air raids, neither Japan nor Germany had bombers that could fly far enough to bomb US cities on the mainland.

Living with the bombs

There were fears that bombing would create mass panic, but most people just carried on with their daily lives. Children went to school, and during air raids slept in air raid shelters instead of bedrooms. Air raids were often at night, so children had to be woken and taken to the shelter when the **sirens** gave the alarm. Many people stayed at home during air raids, while others spent the night in shelters. Thousands slept in Chislehurst Caves in Kent, England, while many Londoners slept in London Tube (Underground) railway stations.

September 1940	1940–1941	1942
The German Luftwaffe begins its bombing raids on London. Known as the Blitz, it reaches its climax in 1941.	Raids on Coventry and many other British cities damage thousands of houses and many schools.	Allied air forces begin round-the-clock bombing of Germany: the RAF by night, the USAAF by day.

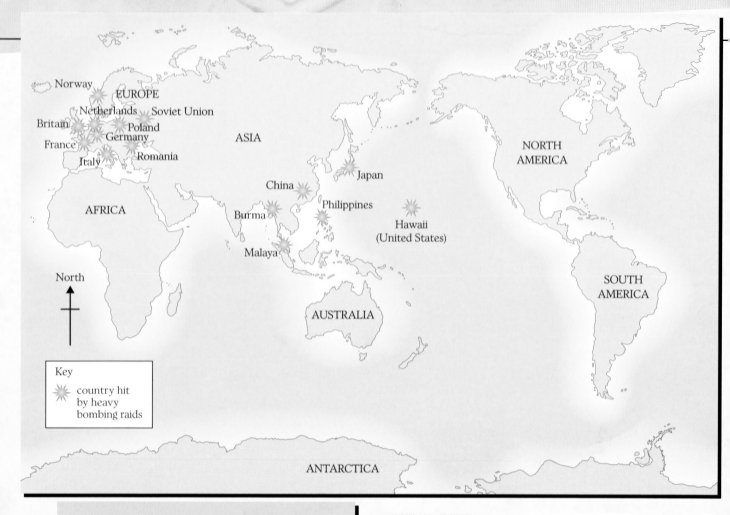

▲ This map shows where the heaviest bombing raids of the war took place.

Raids on Germany

German children experienced the terrors of air raids almost constantly in 1944–1945. In Berlin, people crammed the U-Bahn (underground/subway) stations. With as many as 5,000 people crowded into shelters meant for 1,500, it was very uncomfortable. People lit candles to check if the air was being used up. If a candle on the ground went out, children had to be picked up and held at shoulder height, where there was more oxygen. At times, the air got so bad that everyone had to leave, even while the bombs were still falling.

WWII bombing casualties

Australia	several hundred
Britain	over 60,000
China	over 560,000
Germany	600,000
Japan	over 400,000
Soviet Union	over 500,000
United States	over 2,000 (in Hawaii)

June–September 1944

Britain is hit by German V-1 flying bombs. A new evacuation begins, with over 1 million people moving out of London.

February 1945

Allied air raids on the German city of Dresden kill at least 30,000 people.

6 and 9 August 1945

Two US atomic bombs wipe out the Japanese cities of Hiroshima (over 100,000 killed) and Nagasaki (over 40,000 killed).

What an air raid was like

Children were often in bed when night raiders flew over their homes and began dropping bombs. Some were asleep in public shelters, where people settled down from early evening. Other children were woken, snuggled in overcoats, dressing gowns, and blankets, and taken to the family shelter, usually in the garden. Some children spent the night playing games, reading, or annoying their more nervous parents. Others slept right through the air raid till the "all clear" siren signal told people the bombers had flown away.

After a raid, children came out onto the streets to inspect the damage. They watched rescuers freeing people from collapsed buildings. They might chat to the local Air Raid Precautions (**ARP**) warden, and then sneak off to hunt for souvenirs – bits of bomb casing or, even better, part of a shot-down German plane.

In the News

"'Run, rabbits, run' calls the teacher, and instantly some 20 or 30 little people disappear, beneath the desks …" This was how a British government booklet of 1941 described "The Schools Under Fire". Daytime raids became so common that schoolchildren soon got used to them. According to this **propaganda** booklet, when told to leave the classroom, one boy complained, "Bother, there's that old siren again."

Sounds and smells of an air raid

- First, children heard air raid sirens wailing, then the drone of aircraft engines, the thump of bombs exploding, and crashes as buildings collapsed.

- Children also heard the "boom-boom" of **anti-aircraft guns** firing at the bombers. Afterwards, they walked through rubble and puddles of water from fire-fighters' hoses, and smelled burning wood and explosive (from the bombs).

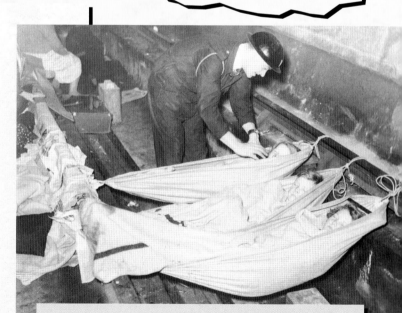

▲ In London, many people sheltered from air raids inside Underground railway stations. In this photo, children are sleeping in hammocks slung between the rails!

AIR RAIDS

◄ This young girl has just been rescued from a bombed house by an ARP warden.

In the News

There were many stories of lucky escapes, often with a funny side. This is an example. A man from Clydeside in Scotland was blown to the ground by a bomb blast while walking home. Picking himself up, he saw what looked like a body, half-buried under rubble. The "body" turned out to be a 14-year-old boy, unhurt but upset because his "good trousers" had been blown off! He was scared his mother would "give him a row" [tell him off].

▼ People on both sides suffered from the misery of air raids. This German woman is holding her baby in a crowded air raid shelter in Wehoff, Germany.

Eyewitness

At first, the British government feared that children would be terrified by air raids. Parents were told to organize games and singsongs to distract children. But one teacher reported that as bombs fell, "the boys were rubbing their hands with glee in expectation of the bomb splinters and souvenirs they would be able to collect."

15

CHILDREN IN OCCUPIED EUROPE

In Europe, millions of children lived for five years under Nazi rule. They went to school, but grew up in an atmosphere of fear and hatred. In Germany, the Nazis believed children should be raised to become Nazis too.

Life under enemy rule

Across Europe, the Nazi occupiers imposed strict laws. People had to stay in after dark, they could not travel from one town to another without permission, and schools could teach only "approved" subjects that agreed with the Nazi view of history and the world. Children who looked "Aryan" (German) were encouraged to become Nazis, but others were persecuted simply because of their race or religion. A few **collaborators** helped the Germans, but most children in **occupied countries** grew to hate the invaders. They hated being cold and hungry, having worn-out clothes, and seeing cruelty everywhere.

Children in Germany

Hitler said, "German youth of the future must be as tough as leather and as hard as steel." German boys joined an organization called the *Jungvolk* (Young Folk) at the age of ten. When they were fourteen, they moved into the *Hitler Jugend* (Hitler Youth). Members of the Hitler Youth were taught Nazi ideas; they behaved like junior soldiers, parading with banners. They were taught to obey Hitler and the Nazis, and trained for fitness through sport, camping, and hiking. Girls joined the *Bund Deutscher Madel* (League of German Maidens, pictured here). They also did keep-fit, and were taught how to be a "good German wife and mother". So-called hooligans belonging to youth gangs were arrested by the police, and the leaders executed.

9 April 1940

German troops invade Norway. In Norway, Vidkun Quisling heads a government that supports Germany, but most Norwegians hate the Nazis.

30 June 1940

German troops invade the Channel Islands, the only British territory to be occupied.

22 June 1941

Germany invades the Soviet Union. The Russians burn houses, machines, and crops as they retreat, so that the Germans cannot use them.

Nazi atrocities

The Nazis acted with great cruelty. Children watched in horror as Jewish friends were taken away, never to be seen again. Thousands of children died in **concentration camps**. Others were murdered; in occupied countries the Nazis sometimes killed everyone in a village as a punishment, in revenge for **Resistance** attacks on Germans.

Resistance

Families in occupied countries listened in secret to radio broadcasts from London by the **BBC**. This is how they got news of the war; the Germans only broadcast propaganda. With help from the Allies, Resistance groups organized a secret war against the occupiers. Some brave children risked their lives to help the Resistance, for example, by carrying messages and helping to hide Allied airmen who had been shot down.

▲ Millions of Europeans suffered under Nazi occupation. These children are pictured waiting for soup in occupied Prague, the capital of Czechoslovakia.

20 July 1941

The BBC begins broadcasting the "V for Victory" tune, "da-da-da-dah", (the Morse code for V) to occupied Europe.

6 September 1941

All Jews over the age of six must wear a yellow Star of David (to show they are Jews), by order of the Nazis.

February–May 1942

Japan conquers and occupies Malaya, Singapore, the Dutch East Indies, and the Philippines.

The plight of Jewish children

For Jewish children, the war held even worse terrors. The Nazis hunted down and exterminated (killed) as many Jews as they could in every occupied country. In Poland, the Nazis shut up all the Jews of Warsaw (Poland's capital) inside a walled district known as the **ghetto**. Inside the ghetto, people starved and got sick, and many died. Some people risked their lives to smuggle in food and medicine.

In July 1942, the Nazis began rounding up ghetto Jews and taking them away to death camps. Mr and Mrs Goldsobel had been in the ghetto since October 1940, with their two daughters, Liliana and Sorela. In September 1942, the Goldsobel family was sent to a camp called Treblinka. There they all died in the **gas chambers**. Sorela was only seven years old. The Goldsobel family had become just four more victims of the Holocaust, the mass murder of around 6 million people during World War II.

Eyewitness

A young woman named Irena Sendler helped smuggle Jewish children out of the Warsaw ghetto. She hid them in potato sacks or in rubbish carts – a mechanic carried one baby in his toolbox. "In my dreams I still hear the cries when they left their parents," she said later.

▲ Jewish children hang from a tram inside the Warsaw ghetto in Poland. Few of them will have survived the war – most were transported to death camps and then murdered, or were killed in the Jewish uprising of 1943.

▶ Jewish children living under Nazi occupation were barred from playgrounds and sports arenas. They had to go to separate schools. All Jews, like this family, had to wear a star sewn on their clothes.

Children in Poland

- To make room for German settlers, the Nazis moved millions of Poles from western Poland.

- Many old people and children died on the journey east.

- Small children who looked "Aryan" were taken away and adopted by German families.

- In October 1940, all the Jews in Warsaw were forced into the ghetto.

▼ Of the 3 million Jews in Poland, most were arrested by the Nazis and taken by train to death camps such as Treblinka and Auschwitz. In these camps, men, women, and children were murdered with poison gas. The Polish Resistance tried to help Jews escape, but only 150,000 managed to survive by hiding.

GROWING UP AT WAR

Life for many children went on much as usual – even if their school roof was blown off by a bomb. Babies learned to walk and talk. Children went to school and played with their friends.

The routine of war

War became routine. Children got used to food rationing, though they missed sweets, and chocolate became a treat. There was a lot of government advice about healthy eating with plenty of vegetables, cheap or free milk, orange juice, and cod-liver oil. The result was that British children were on the whole better fed and healthier than before the war. This was not the case in occupied countries, where many children became thin and ill because of lack of proper food.

Children also became used to air raids. If younger children were sleepy after a disturbed night of bombing, teachers let them have a nap during the day. Reading helped to pass the hours in air raid shelters, and public libraries reported that children were borrowing more books.

▶ Children playing on a bombsite. Bombed buildings were exciting but dangerous playgrounds – unexploded bombs often lay buried under the rubble. Some bombs were still being dug up in London sixty years later!

In the News

In 1942, the first American soldiers began arriving in Britain. Most British children knew about the USA only from films. "We know a great deal about you ... most of the films we see are made in Hollywood," said a leaflet welcoming US servicemen to Britain. US troops were friendly and generous. They often handed out chocolate bars and chewing gum.

1940	13 October 1940	February 1942
The latest Walt Disney films *Pinocchio* and *Fantasia* are cinema treats of the year for children.	Britain's Princess Elizabeth (age 14) broadcasts a radio message to child evacuees. Today she is Queen Elizabeth II.	Two million British children begin swallowing doses of free cod-liver oil, to help improve their health.

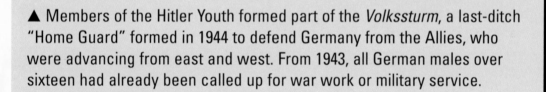

▲ Members of the Hitler Youth formed part of the *Volkssturm*, a last-ditch "Home Guard" formed in 1944 to defend Germany from the Allies, who were advancing from east and west. From 1943, all German males over sixteen had already been called up for war work or military service.

Young people at war

Teenagers could remember what "before the war" was like – when you could buy bananas and oranges, and as much ice cream and chocolate as you could afford. Younger children had only hazy memories of a world without bombers, blackouts, and sudden bangs in the night. Teenagers knew that when they left school they too would be involved in the war, as war workers or servicemen and women. Some talked eagerly of becoming **commandos** or fighter pilots. Many of the RAF fighter pilots who fought in the Battle of Britain in 1940 were only eighteen and nineteen. Thousands of the soldiers who landed in Normandy, France on **D-Day** in 1944 had been at school when the war began.

July 1942	**December 1942**	**August 1944**
Bad news for British children: sweets are now rationed.	School dinners become a permanent part of British school life – previously they were only an emergency measure.	Another mass evacuation programme begins in Britain, after Germans launch flying bombs and rockets.

Wartime toys and games

Toyshops had less to sell in wartime because there were no imported toys from Germany or Japan. Also, some toy factories switched to making war materials. Many children got fewer presents than in peacetime, but children still had fun with home-made toys, such as knitted dolls or wooden aeroplanes. Kites were banned in Britain – in case a high-flying kite should damage an RAF plane, or even be mistaken for an enemy aircraft!

Many toys had a war theme. Small children coloured in painting books with pictures of soldiers, sailors, and airmen. They could also dress dolls in uniform using a kit called "Dolly Joins the Forces". Popular war-themed toys included push-along planes, toy tanks and searchlights, battleships for the bath, and model soldiers. For quieter moments, there were card games, board games, and jigsaws. Hitler made a good joke-target for dartboard games; one called "Plonk" used Hitler's open mouth as the bulls-eye!

▲ War games reflected the times. The most popular games involved soldiers, sailors, warplane pilots, ARP wardens, and nurses.

◀ "Spot the plane" books printed pictures of planes, so that children could tell whether a plane was "one of ours" or "one of theirs". Similar silhouettes appeared on aircraft identification posters in factories and military bases, so the books made children feel grown-up.

GROWING UP AT WAR

◄ Traditional toys were expensive. Toymakers had to find new materials, since rubber, cork, and hemp were scarce. These US children are playing with models made of paper instead of wood, which was needed for the war effort.

Wartime alphabet

"E stands for evacs [evacuees] of various sizes

Who find country life brimful of surprises..."

This was one of the rhymes in a wartime alphabet book for children, called The Defence ABC, *by John Hassall.*

In the News

"A girl's wartime adventure on a lonely Pacific island" was the heading for a typical story in *Girls' Crystal* magazine in 1944. The picture showed two girls confronting Japanese soldiers, with the dramatic caption: "ALONE AGAINST THE INVADERS". Readers were in no doubt who would win.

Eyewitness

"Christmas 1943 was not much good for toys. Most of the ones in the shops were second-hand, but really expensive ..." So British children were glad the Women's Voluntary Service (WVS) ran toy-exchanges, where families could swap toys and books. Children were pleased, because: "Someone else's old toy was new to us. There were even rocking horses, tricycles, and a doll's house. And someone had even bothered to find keys for the wind-up toys."

Item from a WVS news bulletin, 1944

FAMILY LIFE

Family life in wartime was different. Mothers went to work. Fathers were often away for months. Even when the fighting stopped and peace returned, becoming a family again wasn't always easy.

Many families were split up because men (fathers, brothers, and uncles) were away fighting or doing war work. Mothers too were often away at work – many more women worked full-time than before the war. Older sisters left home to join the services or to add their skills to the war effort. Some evacuee children were away from home for years. So were fathers, particularly those held captive as **prisoners of war**. Many, killed in action, did not return at all. Some marriages broke under the strain of wartime separation. Divorce, fairly rare before the war, became more common, and this caused further problems for children.

Children on their own

The war made many children grow up more quickly. They had to look after themselves, and care for younger brothers and sisters while mum was out at work. Some grew up without one or both parents. Some lost brothers and sisters. When servicemen came home in 1945, small children often did not recognize the man who said he was their father.

▶ Children did their bit to help with domestic chores. In the 1940s, it was quite common for parents to send children to the local shop with a basket and shopping list.

December 1940	June 1941	1942
The British government asks people to use less milk and not waste food at Christmas.	Clothes rationing starts in Britain. Factory-made "Utility" clothes are designed to be cheap and hardwearing.	Families are told to grow more food during the "Dig for Victory" campaign.

Having fun as a family

At home, families listened to the radio in the evenings. Children had their own teatime programmes (such as the BBC's *Children's Hour*) and also enjoyed comedy shows and music. Most children also looked forward to a visit to the cinema – "going to the pictures". People kept in touch by letter and visiting, and by telephone if they had one. Few families had cars, and petrol was rationed, so outings had to be by foot, bike, bus, or train. People made the most of Christmases and birthdays, even if they could not buy fancy decorations or sugar-iced cakes. The seaside was still fun when the sun shone, if you could find a beach not closed off for army training or cluttered with "tank-trap" defences against a German invasion.

▲ Parties were still fun, even if mothers found it difficult getting enough sugar and fruit to make birthday cakes! Birthday cards were also smaller during the war, as paper was rationed.

1942
Food and petrol are rationed in the United States. In Britain, people are told not to bath in more than 12.5 cm (5 inches) of water.

October 1942
Cardboard wedding cakes go on sale after the British government bans icing-sugar toppings on cakes.

February 1943
US shoppers are rationed to three pairs of new shoes a year. In Britain, the ration is one pair. All school uniforms in Britain must be grey.

Together again?

In 1945, people celebrated the end of the war with parades and street parties. Millions of men started to come home, and families were reunited. It was a strange time for many children who had grown up during the war. Some were shy of their "strange" fathers; others said crossly, "Mum tells us what to do," and "When are you going back to the army?"

Victory meant peace, but the war had caused global misery. In Germany and Japan, there were no victory celebrations. In those defeated countries, families had been shattered, like their cities. In homes from Moscow to Chicago, many families mourned the loss of someone loved. The world was also learning the horror of the Holocaust in which six million people, many of them children, had been murdered.

Across Europe, millions of people were homeless – displaced by the war. Thousands of families had been separated. Organizations such as the Red Cross worked to reunite parents and children.

▶ British children got used to seeing American and other foreign soldiers, like this American GI. There were men and women from all over the world, and in many uniforms, in wartime Britain.

Countdown to victory

- The Allies invaded France in June 1944. By the winter, they were in Germany.

- The Soviet armies invaded Germany from the east.

- By May 1945, the war in Europe was over.

- In the Pacific, US forces led the Allied advance on Japan, island by island.

- The dropping of two atomic bombs on Japan ended the Pacific war in August 1945.

▶ A US Navy officer arrives home at the end of the war. Meeting up with family after years of separation was not always easy.

Eyewitness

Rosina Smith's son Martin was born in 1941, a month after her soldier husband Steve sailed with the British Army for Singapore. There he was taken prisoner in February 1942. She had no news of him until a letter came in August 1945. Thin and ill with malaria, Steve came home in October 1945. His little son waited shyly at the gate, as the stranger in uniform walked towards the house. The soldier pulled a football from his kitbag, and the little boy started talking.

Eyewitness

"Around 5 p.m. a knock came on the front door ... I thought it was my son's little friends. I said to him 'Go and tell them you can't come out till later on.' He went to the door and then walked up the hall, looked at me, and said 'It's a soldier, Mummy, with a kit-bag. I think it's your husband...'"

British mother Evelyn Hale, remembering her reunion with her husband in June 1945. Her son had been less than a year old when his father went away.

◀ Special camps were set up for Europe's millions of displaced persons – people who had lost homes and families. The war-ravaged continent had become a vast refugee camp. Among the homeless were many children separated from their parents.

PEACE RETURNS

In 1945, people celebrated the end of the war. First in May (VE, or Victory in Europe day), then in August (when Japan surrendered), excited crowds jammed the streets.

Children were treated to open-air street parties, with cakes, sandwiches, and jellies. Music and dancing filled city streets and country villages all day and into the night. A nine-year-old girl later wrote about how exciting it was, saying "I had never seen a street-lamp working or a shop window lit up ..." There would be sweets again, and ice cream.

Then the parties were over, and people went back to work. Schools reopened for the new year. Youngsters looked at notice boards listing the names of former students who had died in World War II – new names beneath older lists of those killed in World War I (1914–1918). What would the world be like after the war? So many children had grown up with war, with its sounds and smells, excitements and fears. Going back to school seemed almost dull. But children knew there was much rebuilding to be done, and they would play their part in it. On VE Day, British prime minister Winston Churchill told his people, "This is your victory ... Everyone, man or woman, has done their best." He might have added that children had done their best, too.

▶ These children in London are making the most of their VE Day celebration party. Peace at last! The younger ones would not have been able to remember a time when there had not been a war on.

TIMELINE

1939

30 August 16,000 children are evacuated from Paris, France.

1 September Germany invades Poland. World War II begins.

3 September Britain and France at war with Germany. Evacuation of children from Britain's cities gets under way.

1940

January People in Britain start to get used to food rationing.

March British professional soccer matches restart after being banned when war began.

April Germany invades Denmark and Norway.

May German armies invade Belgium, the Netherlands, and France. Many children are among the fleeing refugees.

May British boys of 17 can join the new Local Defence Volunteers (later renamed the Home Guard), set up to help the army protect Britain.

May–June A British army is evacuated from Dunkirk, in France.

June France surrenders.

July–September Children in southern England watch planes "dog-fighting" overhead during the Battle of Britain.

September London children experience their first bombs: the Blitz has begun.

1941

March The British government sets up more nurseries for babies and toddlers, so that women can work in factories.

April Germany invades Greece and Yugoslavia.

22 June Germany invades the Soviet Union.

June Clothes rationing begins in Britain.

7 December Japanese attack on Pearl Harbor brings the United States into the war.

1942

February Singapore and the Philippines fall to Japan, which also bombs northern Australia.

February Soap ration in Britain is one tablet per person a month.

March US government interns Japanese-Americans in special camps.

May Start of petrol rationing in the USA.

June The last Jewish schools in Germany are closed by the Nazis.

July Sweets are rationed in Britain.

October The US government freezes wages, rents, and prices. In Britain, the milk ration is cut to 2.5 pints (1.2 litres) a week.

December The British government plans to offer school dinners to all children.

1943

February The Allies begin bombing Germany night and day.

February A German army surrenders at Stalingrad, marking the end of their advance eastwards into the Soviet Union.

May All women between the ages of 18 and 45 in Britain must do at least part-time war work.

July Allies land in Sicily, to begin the invasion of Italy.

1944

January The British government passes a new Education Act, planning post-war education.

April Britain's first prefab homes are built, to replace bombed houses.

6 June D-Day; Allied armies invade France.

12/13 June First German V-1 flying bomb falls on London. New evacuation scheme is put into action to remove children from danger.

25 August Children join the celebrations as the French capital, Paris, is liberated by the Allies.

8 September The first V-2 rocket falls on London.

September Street lights are turned on in Britain as the blackout is eased after five years.

September Allied armies enter Germany. The Nazis form a Home Guard of people aged 16 to 60.

October German bread ration is cut to one loaf a week.

1945

April US troops land on Okinawa, close to Japanese mainland.

30 April Hitler kills himself as Soviet armies close in on Berlin.

7 May Germany surrenders.

8 May VE Day is a day of parades and parties across Britain as children join in the peace celebrations.

6 August The Allies drop an atomic bomb on Hiroshima and another on Nagasaki three days later. The war is soon over.

14 August People celebrate V-J (Victory over Japan) Day.

GLOSSARY

air raid attack by aircraft dropping bombs on cities

air raid shelter building designed to protect people inside from bombs

Allies nations that fought against Japan, Germany, and Italy during World War II

ancestry a person's family background

anti-aircraft guns big guns firing shells thousands of metres into the air to hit or scare off enemy planes

ARP stands for Air Raid Precautions, later changed to Civil Defence. An organization in Britain that dealt with bombs and bomb damage.

Battle of Britain air battle between the Royal Air Force and the German air force or *Luftwaffe* in 1940

BBC British Broadcasting Corporation, which controlled radio in wartime Britain

billeting officer official in charge of finding homes for evacuees

blackout measures to reduce all lights showing at night, to hide possible targets from enemy bombers

Blitz short for *Blitzkrieg*, German for "lightning war". The term is used to describe the German bombing attack on Britain beginning in 1940.

civil war fighting between people who live in the same country

civilian person not in the armed forces

collaborators people who help an enemy invader of their country

commando soldier trained for raiding missions

concentration camp prison in which Jews and other prisoners of the Nazis were kept, in terrible conditions

D-Day name for the Allied invasion of France, on 6 June 1944

evacuation moving people from danger to safer places

evacuees people who were evacuated

gas chamber room in which people were killed by poison gas

ghetto sealed area of a town in which Jews were forced to live

Holocaust Nazi mass murder of Jews and other peoples during World War II

Jews followers of the religion of Judaism

Nazi member of the National Socialist German Workers' Party, led by Adolf Hitler

occupied countries countries invaded and ruled by an enemy during wartime

persecution deliberate cruel treatment

prisoner of war person captured by the enemy during a war

propaganda control of information to show your own side in a good light and the enemy in a bad way

rationing controlling the supply of food and other goods. People were given ration books with coupons in, to use when buying rationed goods.

refugees people forced to leave their homes because of natural disaster, famine, persecution, or war

Resistance groups of people in occupied countries who worked and fought against the enemy

siren a machine used to sound the alarm when enemy bombing planes were approaching

FINDING OUT MORE

If you are interested in finding out more about World War II, here are some more books and websites you might find useful.

Further reading

Your local public library's adult section should have plenty of war books, including books about what it was like to be a child during the war. Written by people who were actually there, such books will give you an idea of what ordinary children thought about the war and their part in it.

Books for younger readers

Britain at War: Air Raids, Martin Parson (Wayland, 1999)

Causes and Consequences of the Second World War, Stewart Ross (Evans, 2003)

Causes of World War II, Paul Dowswell (Heinemann Library, 2002)

Going to War in World War II, Moira Butterfield (Franklin Watts, 2001)

History Through Poetry; World War II, Reg Grant (Hodder Wayland, 2001)

The Day the War was Won, Colin Hymion (Ticktock Media, 2003)

World in Flames: In the Air, Peter Hepplewhite (Macmillan Children's Books, 2001)

World in Flames: On Land, Neil Tonge (Macmillan Children's Books, 2001)

WW2 Stories: War at Home, Anthony Masters (Franklin Watts, 2004)

WW2 Stories: War in the Air, Anthony Masters (Franklin Watts, 2004)

WW2 True Stories, Clive Gifford (Hodder Children's Books, 2002)

Websites

http://www.iwm.org.uk/ – the website of the Imperial War Museum in London.

http://www.wartimememories.co.uk/ – a website containing wartime recollections, including those of children who lived through the war.

http://bbc.co.uk/history/war/wwtwo/ – this website from the BBC has lots of resources about World War II.

INDEX

Titles in the *World At War* series include:

Hardback: 0-431-10376-3

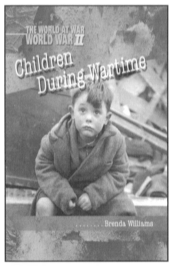

Hardback: 0-431-10380-1

Hardback: 0-431-10377-1

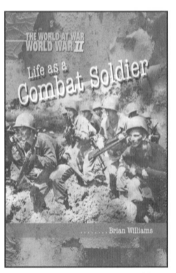

Hardback: 0-431-10378-X

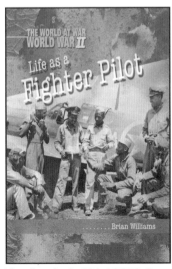

Hardback: 0-431-10379-8

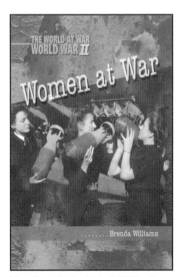

Hardback: 0-431-10375-5

Find out about other titles from Heinemann Library on our website www.heinemann.co.uk/library